POTTY TRAINING
BOOT CAMP
FOR TWINS

POTTY TRAINING BOOT CAMP FOR TWINS

Potty Train Your Twins in Four Days before the Age of Two

Dianne DeLongchamps

iUniverse, Inc.
Bloomington

Potty Training Boot Camp for Twins
Potty Train Your Twins in Four Days before the Age of Two

The information, ideas, and suggestions in this book are not intended as a substitute for professional medical advice. Before following any suggestions contained in this book, you should consult your personal physician. Neither the author nor the publisher shall be liable or responsible for any loss or damage allegedly arising as a consequence of your use or application of any information or suggestions in this book.

iUniverse books may be ordered through booksellers or by contacting:

iUniverse
1663 Liberty Drive
Bloomington, IN 47403
www.iuniverse.com
1-800-Authors (1-800-288-4677)

Because of the dynamic nature of the Internet, any web addresses or links contained in this book may have changed since publication and may no longer be valid. The views expressed in this work are solely those of the author and do not necessarily reflect the views of the publisher, and the publisher hereby disclaims any responsibility for them.

Any people depicted in stock imagery provided by Thinkstock are models, and such images are being used for illustrative purposes only.
Certain stock imagery © Thinkstock.

ISBN: 978-1-4620-2691-3 (sc)
ISBN: 978-1-4620-2692-0 (ebk)

Printed in the United States of America

iUniverse rev. date: 11/11/2011

Cover Art by Betsy Rudolph

CONTENTS

Thank you, my sweet twins, for being the precious children that you are and for giving me the subject matter to write this book.

Part I:
Introduction

Is it possible to successfully potty train twins in four days before the age of two?

Yes it is. *Potty Training Boot Camp for Twins* is a comprehensive step-by-step program that will have your twins potty trained in four days. The system is based on loving and consistent training in conjunction with the use of the American Sign Language "potty" sign, which enables your children to communicate their needs quickly and effectively.

Until the early 1960's when disposable diapers were introduced, most American and European children were toilet trained by eighteen to twenty-two months. It is not our babies' abilities that have changed; it is our way of thinking. Medical research shows that children are mentally and physically ready to complete potty training before the age of two. Even today, most toddlers around the world finish training by age eighteen to twenty-four months.

Trying to stay on top of "giving your child the opportunity" to use the potty on a regular basis with twins is tough, and can extend the training process over several months. This program is designed to consolidate that same training concept into four days. *Potty Training Boot Camp for Twins* will enable you and your twins to quickly transition into a "diaper-free" world!

Why is eighteen to twenty-four months the perfect age?

At this age toddlers are starting to realize their bodily functions, they can walk themselves to and from the potty, they can pull their pants down, and they understand simple requests. They aren't afraid of things yet; therefore, they do not have the fear of pooping in the potty and flushing it away. They haven't hit the headstrong "terrible two's," during which they become incredibly proficient with the word "no." Toddlers who have entered the age range of two to three are famous for their contrariness, and inducing them to say "yes" to anything is difficult. Getting them to relax while doing something they don't want to do is almost impossible. Starting to potty train between the ages of two and three increases the likelihood of a parent-child conflict, and when parents try to force the issue, potty training stalls. At the age of eighteen to twenty-four months, children are still very eager to please, which makes training much easier.

Children who do not start learning until the age of three often face a number of special problems.

- Long-established habits of using the diaper as a toilet are entrenched.
- After having ignored the sensations related to elimination for so many years, many children seem to have greater difficulty identifying these signs.
- After passing waste while walking around in diapers, many children have difficulty figuring out how to work their muscles while sitting down.

- Over half the children ages three and up have occasional or chronic problems with constipation. A single bout during potty training can lead to resistance, refusal, and chronic toileting problems.

Throughout the 1940s to the 1960s, children across America and Europe were consistently toilet trained by eighteen to twenty-two months. It was not until the introduction of disposable diapers in the 1960s, and the "child-oriented" philosophy promoted by Procter & Gamble's spokesperson, that the rationale for potty training in later years began. By 2001 the average age for potty training was thirty-five months for girls and thirty-nine months for boys. For more detailed information and studies on this, please see the research findings section on page 6.

What do I mean by "potty trained"?

Your children will be in big-kid underwear during the waking hours and possibly the nap hours within four days. You will never have to put them in a diaper again. Their bladders need to be ready for nights, and once they are trained during the day, this book will give you guidance for night training. I am not going to tell you that there won't be accidents after they are potty trained, because there will be. This is not a perfect science, and toddlers get busy doing things, and sometimes they forget. Keep in mind that there will be accidents at any age, as it comes with the territory. Whether you train your children to use the potty at eighteen months or four years, there are going to be some challenges along the way. I would certainly rather clean up the accident of a two-year-old than a four-year-old, wouldn't you?

How does the program work?

Potty Training Boot Camp for Twins is a program based on loving and consistent training in conjunction with the use of the American Sign Language "potty" sign. Using the ASL "potty" sign is imperative to the training, as children at this age are much more efficient at communicating quickly through signing than verbalizing their needs. While infants and toddlers have a desire to communicate their needs and wishes, they lack the ability to do so clearly because the production of speech—which requires coordinating the lips, tongue, breath, and vocal cords simultaneously—lags behind cognitive ability in the first months and years of life. Hand-eye coordination is possible in advance of the acquisition of verbal skills, and infants and toddlers can learn to express their needs using simple signs for common words, such as "potty."

The program is a commitment on your part, as it takes four days to complete. You will have to set aside this time in advance, with nothing overlapping. If you can truly commit to four days out of your life to *completely focus* on your little ones, you will never have to use a diaper again.

How will I know my toddlers are ready?

Twins are typically born a little earlier than singletons, so as their mother or father, you need to keep that in mind. You need to decide if they are showing signs of being ready. I am the mother of boy/girl twins born at thirty-six and a half weeks and potty trained before their second birthday. If your children were born with complications and are struggling with developmental milestones, this may work better a little later down the line. You know your babies, so do what you feel is right for them. In Part Two, I have detailed signs to look for when deciding whether or not your children are ready.

My children aren't talking yet.

My babies did not have a large vocabulary when we potty trained, so your children do not need this to complete the program. If you have done any sign language, the ASL sign for "potty" is a must. If not, you can practice the "potty" sign several weeks before you start training, as children quickly catch onto sign language. Your twins *must* become proficient at this sign. I will explain how to teach the sign in Part Two.

I have other children at home.

If you have older or younger children, please have someone take your other children, or at least keep them occupied, for the four days.

What if my children are older?

You can still use the basics of this program, but you will come up against different challenges. Although they will "get it" in the first day or two, you will struggle because they are more independent and headstrong than a younger child, and they may not want to use the potty on a regular basis. The program has been shown to work well up to about twenty-six months, and then you will start battling with the fact that your children understand what you want them to do, but may fight you on it. You will have to use more reasoning and more bribery with older children. It could also potentially take longer than four days to have them consistently using the potty.

What do I need to make this program work?

1. Your children must meet *all* of the "I'm ready to learn" signs and the external signs outlined in Part Two.
2. Your children must be completely comfortable using the sign for potty.
3. A full commitment of four days for your children with no outside interference is essential.
4. You need someone to help you during the day with any other children you have.
5. An "I won't give up!" attitude to carry you through day four is required.
6. You need the energy of a Duracell bunny, and the patience of a saint!

Each of these points is key to your success!

Interesting Statistics and Research on Potty Training

Global: Parents throughout the world put babies on small potties for short periods of time as soon as they can sit up by themselves. By making the time spent on the potty enjoyable, parents help the youngsters overcome any fear they might have of the toilet. Parents reward their babies' occasional successes with smiles and applause, which delight little ones even if they don't understand what all the excitement is about. Over time, they come to accept potty training as readily as mealtime, naptime, bath time, and bedtime. As soon as they can walk, parents steer them to the potty for regular practice sessions. When they master the mechanics of buttons and zippers and can get their clothes off and back on by themselves, they are fully trained. As a result, most toddlers around the globe finish training by ages eighteen to twenty-four months.

Historical: In the early 1900s, toilet training was introduced when infants were two to three months old by holding little handheld pots under their bottoms and making a special sound when the baby eliminated. Over time, infants became conditioned to the sound and feel of the pot touching their bottoms and would respond by pushing to relieve themselves. In the 1940s, with the introduction of the automatic washing machine, parents began waiting to introduce the potty until infants could sit up by themselves. Still, the norm was for children to finish potty training by ages one and a half to two. Through the 1950s and into the early 1960s, this trend continued, with most American and European children toilet trained by eighteen to twenty-four months. But in 1961, Procter & Gamble introduced the first disposable diapers. Procter & Gamble's spokesperson, Dr. T. Berry Brazelton, recommended a "child-oriented" approach focused on not starting to teach until the child wanted to learn—and backing off immediately if an initially eager child became bored with the project. He pushed the idea that starting training too early could cause psychological damage to the child and create long-term toileting problems. By 1997, according to a University of Pennsylvania School of Medicine study, only 4 percent of children were trained by age two, with 60 percent trained by three years, and 98 percent out of diapers by their fourth birthday. Today's size-six diaper fits children thirty-five pounds and over. Children are training later and later, as they feel little discomfort when in disposable diapers. In 2001, according to a study reported in *Ambulatory Pediatrics*, the average age for completing potty training in America rose to thirty-five months for girls and thirty-nine months for boys.

Financial: With twins you will go through approximately eight thousand diapers in the first year. You will go through approximately five thousand diapers in the second year. If you are using disposable diapers, at thirty cents per diaper, you have spent approximately four thousand dollars in the first two years of their lives on diapers, and that doesn't include diaper pail liners, wipes, and the little bags you throw the dirty diapers in! If your twins don't train until late into their third year, they can go through up to twenty thousand diapers, costing six thousand dollars. At four years, the cost of diapering your twins would be approximately eight thousand dollars.

Health and hygiene: Contrary to what television ads have led parents to believe, disposables do not keep children "clean and dry." They keep them filthy and dry. Diaper rash, a disorder that was once a telling sign of parental neglect, used to affect about 7 percent of babies. Now that 94 percent of children in the United States wear disposables, diaper rash afflicts 78 percent. Having children "wear their waste" for years on end is a definite health hazard. In fact, most of the illnesses that rage through daycare centers and nurseries are caused by E. coli, the bacteria from fecal contamination. Giardia and rotavirus are also spread through human waste.

Chemicals used to manufacture disposables also leak from wet diapers and are absorbed through the skin. When changing diapers, parents commonly find globs of the superabsorbent gel on their children's genitals. Many parents report allergic reactions, and some say that disposables have triggered asthma attacks in susceptible children.

Delaying potty training is also associated with more frequent urination and can result in other health problems. Because children don't routinely push when peeing until they are being potty trained, they do not exercise their muscles and may not completely empty their bladder. The results of not fully emptying the bladder range from chronic infections to unstable bladders.

The rise of male infertility and increased incidence of undescended testicles in little boys have coincided with the widespread use of disposables. A team of researchers leading the study "Scrotal temperature is increased in disposable plastic lined nappies" (Partsch et al. 2000) believes that disposable diapers may play a role. By containing body heat along with the drips and puddles, disposables raise the temperature of the testicles and scrotum. Prolonged temperature elevation during childhood has been associated with infertility later in life.

Environmental: To acquire the wood pulp for disposable diapers, one billion trees worldwide are cut down per year. What is done to that wood is even more detrimental to us and our world. For every baby diapered with single-use diapers for a two-and-a-half-year period, over two tons of waste is generated. Disposable diapers make up the third largest single consumer item in our waste system—following newspapers and fast food and beverage containers. They account for nearly 4 percent of the total amount of solid waste, and 30 percent of the non-biodegradable waste, and since discarded diapers contain untreated waste, astronomical quantities of raw sewage are dumped into the earth. The major environmental issue surrounding cloth diapers concerns increased air and water pollution. Because cloth diapers are reused, they require laundering, which uses water, heat for the water, and chemicals for cleaning. Cloth diapers put an increased strain on our water sewage system. However, cloth diapers ensure that human waste gets to where it can be treated properly (in a water treatment plant) rather than placed in a landfill where it will take centuries to decompose and potentially spread harmful viruses.

For more information on the impact of diapers please visit:
www.realdiaperassociation.org/diaperfacts.php
www.borntolove.com/e-concerns2.html
www.cleanair.org

Research findings: A review of research reported in the official scientific journal of the American Academy of Pediatrics, *Pediatrics,* turns up a number of startling findings. Experts have established that infants possess the physical capability to delay elimination and respond to cues to use a potty as early as two or three months old.

Max Maizels, professor of urology at Northwestern University's medical school and the attending urologist at Children's Memorial Hospital in Chicago, stated in a 1993 article in *Current Problems in Pediatrics* that by the end of infancy, children can sense bladder fullness and have the muscle skills necessary to postpone urination. Timothy Schum, a toilet training researcher, supplied evidence that led Maizels to conclude that children with a mental age of twenty-one months are ready to *finish* training. By then, most toddlers can remove their clothes and handle the mechanics of the potty by themselves.

In an article published in 2000 titled "Changes in the Toilet Training of Children During the Last Sixty Years: The Cause of an Increase in Lower Urinary Tract Dysfunction?" researchers E. Bakker and J. J. Wyndaele concluded that to avoid permanent bladder dysfunction, parents should start training when children stay dry during the afternoon nap.

Another large study also provides compelling evidence for a link between training and long-term toileting problems. Writing in the *Scandinavian Journal of Urology and Nephrology* in 2001, E. Bakker reported the results of a questionnaire evaluating different aspects of personal and familial situations. All of the youngsters who had bladder problems at age eleven had started training after age two. Factors that resulted in delayed training included allowing children to proceed at their own pace rather than conducting regular potty sits, letting children sip and snack throughout the day, and dressing them in disposable products rather than cloth.

Ironically, Brazelton's own study, which appeared in *Pediatrics* in 1962, showed that one-third of children who didn't stop bed-wetting until age three and a half had started training early. But viewed from that perspective, two-thirds of the children who didn't stop bed-wetting until age three and a half were late starters, and most had begun training after twenty-four months. Of the children who continued to wet and soil after age five, only 12.5 percent had started training before eighteen months of age. The vast majority (87.5 percent) had started training after twenty-four months.

Best-selling author, national columnist, and family therapist John Rosemond has responded to the epidemic of wetting and soiling among older children by recommending a return to the age-old practice of potty training newly mobile toddlers. He points out that early learning does not turn children into emotional basket cases, scar them psychologically, or lead to years of bed-wetting and accidents, as Brazelton suggests. Harsh, insensitive training methods do that.

My Personal Story

When I look back, I realize my daughter was ready to potty train at eighteen months. She would grab her diaper when she urinated and squat when she had a bowel movement. She would look right at me, letting me know what she was doing. Taking into consideration the advice from most of my friends and family, I thought she was too young to start training. At twenty-one and a half months, I purchased two potties, just to start practicing. By twenty-two months, my son was using the potty as often as I would take the time to let him, both to urinate and to have bowel movements. My daughter was not as interested. I felt I had missed the "window" with her that some tell you to watch for. By twenty-three months, my son was starting to lose interest, and so was I! It is tough trying to stay on top of "giving your child the opportunity" to use the potty on a regular basis, especially with two at the same time. I saw myself, along with my children and my husband, becoming lazy with the training, and I realized I needed to do something quickly.

I began my search for some guidance on potty training twins by reading numerous articles, research findings and books on potty training, but there was *nothing* specific to twins. Per the information I gathered, it was clear to me that my toddlers were at an age that was appropriate for potty training. I was confident in their ability to communicate their needs with me, as we had been using American Sign Language since they were six months old. If they could effectively communicate with me via signing when they wanted "more" or "cookies" or "crackers" or "milk", or when they were "all done", how would that help them communicate with me in potty training? I implemented the "potty" sign into our daily routine, and they quickly responded by using the sign during potty and changing times. Another question that kept entering my mind was: Does potty training have to drag on for months? Some articles I read suggested you could potty train a child in a couple of days. What if I integrated the "potty" sign with a power course on potty training? This is how the concept for *Potty Training Boot Camp for Twins* was born. When my twins were twenty-three and a half months old I was able to schedule a long weekend to work with them, and successfully start and complete *Potty Training Boot Camp for Twins*. By the end of day three, both of my children were using the potty on a regular basis and staying dry at nap time, and there was never a diaper in our home again.

Part II:
Potty Training Boot Camp

Congratulations, you have made a wonderful decision to potty train your twins in four days. You are going to be so proud of yourself and your babies, and all of your friends and family will be amazed! Just a little piece of advice: don't make the mistake I made and tell a lot of people you are doing this. You will be beaten up before you start! Trust me, when I told my family, friends, husband—even my mother—I got, "You are crazy," "Good luck," "Let me know how it turns out," and "Don't beat yourself up if it doesn't work." My husband said, "I can't believe you are giving yourself so much brain damage this weekend!" So I would highly recommend keeping this as low-key as possible on the conversation front, except with your spouse/partner and your nanny/childcare provider. You should have your partner's support; and you pay your childcare provider, so she should accept your decision at face value. Some people will think you are crazy, but if you stick with it and do not get frustrated, your little ones will be potty trained in four days or less. When you are *done* with the training and can say, "My children are potty trained!" it is time to start sharing your children's amazing accomplishment with others.

Make Sure Your Toddlers Are Mentally and Physically Ready

Watch your children, not the calendar, for the following "I'm ready to learn" signs:

- Imitating your toileting
- Communicating verbally or with sign language other sensations, such as hunger
- Understanding simple requests, such as "Go get the ball"
- Understanding key concepts, such as the difference between wet and dry
- Beginning to pull diapers off when wet or soiled, or coming to tell you they're dirty
- Following you to the bathroom, showing curiosity, and/or trying to imitate
- Pulling clothes off (at least pants down)
- Climbing onto the potty chair or toilet
- Having dry spells or staying dry for at least two hours
- Occasionally waking from naps dry
- Having regular and well-formed bowel movements
- Investigating their body equipment

Watch your children for the following external signs that show they feel the pressure inside.

- Peering into diaper
- Squatting
- Grabbing diaper
- Crossing legs
- Grunting and grimacing
- Retreating to the corner or behind the couch

About to go: retreating to quiet place, stopping play, quieting down, and squatting.

Going: grabbing diaper, grunting, and crossing legs.

Gone: peering at diaper bulge, sensing different feel, resuming play, and verbalizing production.

These signs tell you that your toddlers are developmentally mature enough to be aware of what's going on inside their body. Your children *must* meet *all* of these guidelines to accomplish this program. If your children do not show these signs by twenty-two to twenty-four months, you may want to consult with your pediatrician.

Let's Get Prepared

The commitment: First and foremost, you must be prepared for this commitment. You must *not* schedule anything for these four days, including errands, phone calls, conference calls, e-mails, coffee with friends, playdates, etc. I would even recommend having a fifth day free just in case one of your babies needs a little extra time. Put your autoresponder on your e-mail and a personal message on your cell that you will be unavailable. You will be at home and/or in your backyard for four days, so mentally prepare for it. Look around your home and figure out the best place to keep your children contained so that you can always keep them within eyesight. Make sure it is an area that you can cover or wipe up easily and where accidents won't cause irreversible damage. Have meals prepared or plan to order out. Have all the laundry done. You must have complete focus on your children during every moment of this program.

Day care: Although I don't recommend sharing what you are about to do with a lot of people, if your children are in day care or you have a nanny, you need to have a sincere discussion with your childcare provider regarding what you are doing and what your goals are. They are going to have to be on board, because after the training, your children will need continued support from those around you and the people who provide them with day-to-day care. Give them this book to review, and get a commitment from them to support you and your children. Although your children will be potty trained in four days, they will need extra attention regarding potty times for the next few weeks to keep them on track.

If your children are in a full-time daycare program, and you and your spouse both work, try to keep them at home for a week if at all possible. It is not necessary, but a little extra time for getting the potty down is better than throwing them back into the classroom after four days at home. I highly recommend getting support from your spouse, friends, or other family members to help you keep them near their comfort zone at home for a week. They can get used to some outings with you — going to the grocery, going to the park, interacting with other children — while you keep a watchful eye on them and remind them of potty time. This will give them some time to get used to being away from home while still remembering to use the potty.

Starting fresh: Depending on the age of your children and how much potty training you have been doing, you might want to give training a break. Your children should at least know what a potty is for. Whether they use it on a regular basis or not, they need to know what you do with it. If you have trained for a while, I would take a couple weeks off to get rid of the old habits and start new ones. Unless they request the potty, don't push it. Just let it go for a while so they can start fresh. Lose any modesty that you may still be clinging onto after giving birth, and *show* your twins what you do on the potty. Let them watch you and help you flush. Have some fun with it, exclaiming, "Yeah, Mommy went potty! I am such a *big* girl!"

The "potty" sign: When starting the training process, it is important to simultaneously say the word "potty" and sign "potty." (Please see illustration on page 18.) Hold your hand up, palm facing forward. Fold your thumb in and place it between your index and middle finger. Fold your fingers down into a fist. The tip of your thumb should be sticking out of the fist between your fingers. Move your wrist back and forth from left to right. You've got it! Every time your children look at the potty or sit on the potty, talk to them about the potty while you sign. When your twins go potty in their diapers or you change their diapers, talk to them about the fact that they peepeed or poopood in their diaper, and use the potty sign. *This takes constant repetition, getting down to their level with eye contact, and using it every time you get the chance.* Every time you use the toilet, make it an opportunity to teach your children by saying, "Look, Mommy is using the potty!" while signing "potty." When you change their diaper, say, "Look, you went peepee," while using the sign. If you know they are about to poop in their diaper, say, "Oh, you are going potty," while signing "potty" and looking them in the eye. Get down to their level so that they really see the sign and start to associate their going to the potty in their diaper with the potty in the bathroom and the use of the sign.

American Sign Language "potty" sign.

Schedules: Limit any changes in typical schedules and don't do any traveling for at least a month after training. You want to keep your little ones on track, and change can upset and distract your child and cause accidents. Some children breeze through a change, others don't. Although my son caught on quickly and rarely had any accidents, we traveled to Texas to see family a couple weeks after training, and he started having regular accidents when we returned home. We took a day and really focused on the potty again, and he was totally back on track. Although my daughter typically had a little more of a struggle with the potty, she was perfect in Texas and had no problem adjusting there or when we returned. If setbacks occur, they can easily be addressed.

Boot Camp Supplies and Rations

Potties: Invest in two potty chairs with soft cushioned seats, as well as potty seats for the adult toilets that your twins might be using soon. I recommend simple potties, not the ones that make noise, light up, or change colors—these have too much going on and take away from the focus of the training. Purchase sturdy, durable potty chairs with stable bases that won't tip over when your children get up to check progress. Remove the urine guards for little boys for now. They get in the way and can scratch your children and scare them. A portable potty for the weeks after you train and are out and about is recommended. You can keep it in the car or in your diaper bag. It is a wonderful thing to have! We traveled with one for road trips, camping, long outings to the park, etc., until my twins were three and a half. They have a couple of choices at the larger baby supply stores.

Unscented wipes, booty cream, dish towels, and vinegar: I recommend toddler wipes that are actually flushable. If not, you can just use toilet paper, and take care of a final booty wipe with a baby wipe and toss it in the trash. Unscented wipes are preferable because they will cause less irritation than the scented ones. Your children may get a bit of a rash with the change from diapers to cotton underwear and all of the wipes they will experience during potty training. Booty cream will help with that. Dish towels and vinegar water make for a good cleanup on wood floors and carpet.

Underwear: You will need at least twenty to thirty pairs for each child, and make them the fun ones with cartoon and movie characters all over them! Purchase some of the thicker training underwear as well, along with the training pants with the plastic on the outside. I used these for naps. This is a minimum, and you will have to do at least one load of laundry while they nap. I know this sounds crazy, but they aren't used to controlling their urges at this point, so they will go through a lot of undies in the first couple of days. I also recommend nighttime Pull-Ups until they are consistently waking up dry in the morning (and please call them "nighttime undies," *not* "diapers").

Toys, movies, stickers, and books: Your local library and dollar stores are great places to get started for these supplies. Get lots of board books – the smaller the better – as your children will enjoy looking at them while sitting on the potty. Sit between your twins and read to them while they are on the potty before naps and bedtime. Potty training books are fun, but not necessary. They reinforce the actions that you are teaching them, and children seem to enjoy them. Stickers are fun to put either in a book or on the potty top when they finish using it. Crayons, chalk, water colors, drawing paper, Legos, movies, interactive toys, outside toys, puzzles, musical toys (such as kazoos, tambourines, and horns), hats, crowns, tiaras, Play-Doh, silly things (such as sticky crawlers)—use *anything* to keep you and your children entertained for four days. I stocked up with supplies from the library and the dollar store so that I had new items to rotate out each day. A camping tent and a tunnel are great fun, and they are easy to hose out.

Food and beverage: You will need to get your children to drink lots of liquids so that they can get a lot of practice. I used a combo of one-third juice and two-thirds water throughout the day. Most kids love juice, but I like to dilute it, as it is high in sugar content. Salty things make them thirsty, thus giving more opportunities for the potty. Make sure to have plenty of snacks on hand: pretzels, goldfish, raisins, dried fruit, apples, and peanut butter. I recommend special treats, like gummy bears, M&M's, and dried fruit, after your babies actually accomplish a pee or poop on the potty. You will also want food prepared for your family's lunch and dinner. You won't want to cook during the training process.

Patience, humor, a positive attitude, and complete commitment: These are the keys to a successful process. You must accept that for four days you will be solely committed to potty training your children. If you work, let everyone know you will be taking this time off, and have someone cover your business. If you have other children, have someone take them for those four days. This program becomes mentally challenging by day three. Just remind yourself how fantastic it will be when your twins are potty trained. If you start to feel negative, shake it off. Take anything positive that you have seen out of either of your children and focus on that. If by day two they have even *once* told you that they need to go potty, *they get it*! And if you have made it to day three, you can make it to day four. A lot of people want to give up on day three. Don't give up! And don't lapse back to the diaper! Throw those things away the day you start, and don't have any in the house. For those of us who went "cold turkey" with the bottles and pacifiers, it is the same thing. If you don't have them in the house, it is unlikely that you will drive to the store to get replacements.

Two-Week Countdown

Don't push any training at all. If you don't have potties yet, go out and get two simple potties with soft seats, and set them in the bathroom that you use the most.

Focus on showing them what you do on the potty. These are your babies. Lose the modesty and show them what goes on in the potty! "Yeah, Daddy is peepeeing! Yeah, Mommy is pooping! Mommy is so big!" Clap, sing, and get excited for yourself. "Can you help me flush the potty? Bye-bye, peepee!

Bye-bye, poopoo!" Children are inquisitive, and they want to do what you do. Daddy, if you are training, please sit on the potty when showing your babies how to use it; standing will just confuse them.

Communicate with them. Make sure that you have your children's attention when you are talking to them. Look them in the eye and tell them, "We are going to start wearing big-kid undies soon. Won't that be fun? We aren't going to wear baby diapers anymore, because we are going to learn to peepee and poopoo on the potty like Mommy." "See your potties? Won't they be fun to use?" If they want to use the potty, let them. Be totally supportive, and get excited, but don't push them to use it.

Make sure they know the sign for "potty." By now your toddlers should be using the sign for potty on a regular basis. It is much easier for young toddlers to sign than to use their words. Signing enables children to communicate their needs much more efficiently than using their vocabulary. This will be extremely important during training. *Do not start the training until your children are proficient in using the American Sign Language "potty" sign.*

Finish gathering your supplies. Finalize your supplies noted in the "Boot Camp Supplies and Rations" section so you aren't running around like a crazy person the day before you start training. Prepare soups, casseroles, and frozen meals, and have sandwich ingredients available for all of your meals during the program. I would go ahead and get the portable potty now as well. It will make the days and weeks after potty training so much easier for you and your babies.

Locate your base camp. Figure out where you are going to locate your base camp during the training process. This should be a relatively contained area so that you can see your children at all times. Other than nap time and bedtime, this is where you will spend the four days of the program. If you have hardwood floors on the main level, plan on keeping your babies there. If you have carpet throughout, create a contained area, and protect the floors with plastic. Make sure you pick up all of the supplies to cover your carpets. It is also nice to make a comfy area for relaxing/reading with sleeping bags and/or blankets that can be washed. A thin water-resistant outdoor play/picnic blanket works well as added protection.

Try to understand their pooping schedule. This will help you know when to schedule a couple minutes on the potty. If your child consistently poops after breakfast or an afternoon snack, those are the times to jot down in your memory.

Two-Day Countdown

Make a special trip with your babies to pick out their own underwear, and make it a very exciting day! There are so many to choose from: the Princesses, Nemo, Elmo, Cars, the Wiggles, Thomas the Train, Dora, Sesame Street, etc. Remember to get plenty of them and make it a big deal!

Start to mentally process your commitment. You will have four homebound days of continually running your children to the potty, putting dry undies on them, and cleaning up pee and poop. You need to be at peace with the fact that you will have to practice true patience and unconditional love while you go through this process. Put a sign on your refrigerator or in your laundry room, or both, that states, "I will not give up!" and say it to yourself every day of your Potty Training Boot Camp.

Potty proof your home. Make sure to put away any beloved rugs and cover any furniture that your children may sit on during the next few weeks. There are going to be accidents, so if there are things in your home that will be ruined or cause you to get upset about if peed on, move them out of the areas they will be spending time in.

Day One: Get Your Marching Boots On!

Are you smiling? You have to be smiling for this to work! Get up and take care of your morning routine. Shower, get dressed, have coffee/juice and breakfast. If there is any last-minute thing you have to do, get it done this morning. Have your family's lunch ready to go. Put a shirt on the babies, and if it is chilly, put a T-shirt and sweatshirt on, but no pants.

Place the potties within a couple of feet of where you are going to be for the day. Make sure to have plenty of paper towels and wipes ready. The shorter the distance to the potties, the better for training, so do not put them in the bathroom.

Communicate with your twins, and tell them that today is a special day! Have your babies help you get all of the diapers in your home and pull them over to the trash can. Make a big deal about throwing them away. "We are going to say 'bye-bye' to our diapers, and we are going to start wearing our big-kid undies! You two are so big!" Cheer, clap, and get excited! Pull their diapers off, throw them into the trash can, and say, "Bye-bye, diapers. Let's put our big-kid undies on! Won't that be fun?" Let them pick out the undies they want to start with, put them on, and get ready for the next few crazy days.

Remember to offer your children plenty of liquids so that they will need to use the potty as much as possible. Let them drink as much as they want to on their own, but don't force it.

Pretzels and crackers with peanut butter for snacks will keep them thirsty.

Today your goal is to keep your children running to the potty as many times as possible, showing unbridled excitement every time. This will start the process of associating the urge to urinate and have a bowel movement with sitting on the potty. This will become exhausting, trust me, but repetition is the key to the program. Keep your eyes closely on them. As soon as they start to pee, run them to the potty and plop them on, saying, "Let's go to the potty! Yeah! You went peepee on the potty. You are so big!" Sign "potty" each time you say it. Clap, jump up and down, shake the tambourine, make up a potty song, give them a sticker to stick on the potty, and just make a big deal out of it. I mean a *crazy* big deal about it! A song can be really simple: "Sarah went peepee (poopoo) on the potty, Sarah went peepee on the potty, Sarah went peepee on the potty, yeeeeeeeeaaaaaah, Sarah!" For my babies, I would just make it into a crazy cheer with a tambourine, flute, or mariachi to add to the tune. They loved it. Put some new undies on them, saying "Okay, let's put some dry undies on," and get ready for the next opportunity. This will be a repetitive process.

Each time they start peeing or pooping, take their hands and get them to the potty as quickly as possible. Do not carry them, as they need to learn to use their little legs to get them to their final destination. Every time you help them to the potty, use the "potty" sign while saying, "Let's go to the potty!" As soon as you get them to the potty, pull those undies off as quickly as you can and try to get them to finish peeing on the potty, praising them the whole way. Again, while they are finishing on the potty, use the potty sign at their eye level while stating, "You are peepeeing in the potty. You are so big!" Now, the technique for poopy undies is a bit different. Sit your child on the potty, carefully pull the back of the undies down until you can get the little poop to roll out into the toilet, and then, in the most excited tone you can muster, sing the praises of how your child has just pooped in the potty, while using the potty sign. "Yeah, sweetie, you just pooped in the potty. You are so big! Oh my goodness, look at that poop! Do you see it? Wow! Do you want to flush it down? Bye-bye, poopoo!" Then carefully pull those undies off and put clean ones on. Now, I hate to get down and dirty, but if that poop is not solid, enabling the "rollout effect," just carefully remove the undies from your child, and rinse them in the potty, acting just as excited as you would if they had actually pooped in the potty. Some of these undies may be worth saving with a quick rinse; some may not. When you contemplate trying to save the ones that really aren't worth messing with (literally!), just remind yourself how much money you are going to be saving in diapers, and let that sucker go! I have tossed my fair share of poopy undies in the first month of my daughter's training, as she was a bit challenging on that front. Hopefully you won't encounter the accident I had when I didn't think my little girl had pooped in her undies yet. I quickly whipped them off to get her on the potty in time, and that nicely deposited poop landed on top of my foot and oozed between my toes! Ugh! It can be messy, but keep the end goal in mind.

After lunch, try to limit your toddlers' liquid intake forty-five minutes to an hour before their nap so that they have potential to stay dry during their nap. I used the training undies (thicker cotton) with the training pants (plastic) over them. Some "potty training advisers" believe that you need to let them nap with just regular undies, and after they wet themselves a few times they get it. I opted for the uninterrupted nap time with some protection. You need to do what you feel is best for you and your children. In my world, a nap is nonnegotiable, and it gives you and your children time to recoup. As a mother of twins, I know how we all dream of that quiet time while our children are sleeping. It won't be long before they will consistently stay dry during their naps and you can lose the training pants. Put them on the potty right before nap time while reading a short little book, and then put them to bed. They may wake up wet; they may wake up dry. If they are dry, make a *huge* deal about it. Tell them how *big* they are to stay dry! Either way, put them on the potty immediately after getting them out of bed, and say, "Let's go peepee." If they are dry they may use it; if they are wet, they probably won't. Put them in dry underwear, and start the process again, running them to the potty each time they start peeing or pooping.

In the evening after dinner, limit their liquid one to one and a half hours before bedtime. Our night consisted of: potty, dinner, potty, bath, read, potty, and bedtime. We changed our routine a bit and read downstairs on the hardwoods with a blanket underneath us. Then we tried the potty one more time and put on our "nighttime undies" (Pull-Ups) and headed to bed. If after bath time you are totally exhausted, give yourself a break, put the nighttime undies on, and call it a day. If you have the energy to plop them on the potty right before lights-out, do so. If not, don't kill yourself. Our focus right now is to get the daytime under control and the concept down.

In review, day one is truly about getting your children used to the idea that when they start to relieve themselves, they land on the potty. Let them get the concept of the urge associated with the potty, and reward them (and yourself!) with praise and hugs this first day. Show them how exciting it is to run to the potty and how "big" they are for doing this. On day two, you can start rewarding them with gummy bears, stickers, M&M's, or anything else that would be a special treat for your child.

Day one will also be about you getting a good grasp of how many minutes it takes them to pee after they drink liquid (usually thirty to forty-five minutes) and when they typically poop. My children usually pooped right after breakfast and then right after lunch or dinner, so we always took a potty break at those times. Every time they start to pee, run them to the potty and plop them on the seat, constantly cheering them on. Put them on the potty briefly before and after they eat and sleep. Always explain to them what you are doing. For example, "It's time for our nap. Let's sit on the potty and go peepee so we will be dry when we wake up." Read a short board book to them, and see if they will relax enough to go poop on the potty after their meals. Do *not* make them sit for extended periods of time on the potty to try to get them to pee or poop. I would never recommend keeping your child on the potty for more than a couple of minutes, and if they don't want to sit on it, *never* force them to. Just give it a break until the next opportunity. The goal is to teach them to associate the urge to pee or poop with running to the potty and sitting on it at that moment.

Get some sleep, because tomorrow starts another very similar day!

Day Two: Give Me a Sign, Please!

Yippee, a new day at Potty Training Boot Camp begins! You are one day closer to a "diaper-free" world, so start your day with a smile. Day two will be very similar to day one. Try to get up and dressed before your little ones rise, or know that you will have to wait until nap time to take care of yourself. Get mentally prepared for another hectic and draining day, and stay strong on your commitment to have your twins potty trained by the end of boot camp. Look at yourself in the mirror and repeat, "I can do it, I can do it, I can do it!"

Have some different books, movies, activities, and simple arts and crafts lined up for today. When your babies wake up, take them to the potty immediately, with the same enthusiasm that you had the day before. "Let's take our nighttime undies off and go peepee in the potty!" Don't mention the fact that they probably woke up wet, because staying dry at night is not part of the program yet. They probably peed in their Pull-Ups right when they woke up and won't use the potty at the moment, but you are just getting them used to their new routine. Put on their big girl/boy undies, and start your day. Remind them, "Tell Mommy when you need to use the potty," while showing them the potty sign again. Just like yesterday, each time your children start to relieve themselves, run to the potty and plop them on, stating, "Let's go to the potty." Remember to repeat the word *and* the sign for "potty" every chance you get. Focus on keeping the good energy going by singing, dancing, clapping, and telling them how proud you are of them and how big they are to go to the potty.

On day two, one or both of your children may start signing or saying "potty" when they begin to relieve themselves, and if so, pile on tons of praise. They may start signing or saying "potty" in the middle of peeing or pooping, or when they finish. This may not occur until day three or four, but it *will* happen. If it happens today, even once, this is a huge accomplishment. Your child is starting to associate the feeling of peeing or pooping with the word/sign "potty" and trips to the potty.

Day two is a good day to start with treats when even a partial pee or poop is accomplished on the potty. It is okay to give them a treat if they start before they land on the potty but finish on the potty. If either of your babies has a consistent schedule on the pooping front, today would be a good day to use that knowledge and plop him briefly on the potty at the typical pooping time and say, "Let's go poop!" Then sit yourself on the adult potty, scrunch up your face, and make grunting pooping noises to see if your little one will imitate you. If not, tell your baby, "What a great try!" and carry on with your day. Keep in mind that thirty seconds later he might poop in his pants, but address that with a quick jaunt to the potty. "Okay, let's finish on the potty! I bet next time you will make it to the potty in time because you are such a big boy!" Today is also a good day to start asking your children, "Do you need to go potty?" Continue to firmly yet happily state, "Let's go potty!" before and after meals and bedtime.

When you run your children to the potty while pee is streaming down their legs or poop has landed in their undies, and plop them on, continue with the praises and celebration. If they halt in midpee or midpoop to tell you what they are doing, praise what they did, not what they didn't do. Run them to the potty and say, "You almost did it. You are so big! Mommy is so proud of you! Let's finish on the potty. What a big kid you are!" When they are actually sitting on the potty and choose to pee or poop, make it a celebration for all. *Everyone* gets a treat/sticker when someone uses the potty, but praise the one who has accomplished the action. Have each child participate in the excitement of their sibling using the potty for true positive reinforcement on all fronts. When family comes home, or a friend comes over to visit or help during the potty training process, make sure you praise your children and tell everyone that they are using the potty and how *big* they are. "See Max and Emily's big kid undies and their potties. How cool are those, Daddy?" "Can you show Grandma your Nemo undies?" "Can you show your big sister your princess undies?" Make sure family members and friends praise your babies on their accomplishments.

One thing that you may struggle with on day two or day three is the fact that one twin will probably catch on faster than the other. By day two, my son was dry during his nap and throughout the day, signing and saying "potty, Mommy" when he needed to go. By day two, my daughter was still using her underwear most of the time. (I know this is contrary to the popular belief that girls are easier to potty train than boys. Hence, the missed "window of opportunity" I commented on earlier comes into play.) I became a little frustrated at this but stayed positive and committed. If this happens in your world, just sit down, regroup, stay positive and consistent, and keep doing what you have been doing. Your second will catch on by the fourth day.

In review, day two is very similar to day one, as you are continuing to reinforce the urge to pee or poop in the potty. It takes a lot of repetition and using the word and sign for "potty" every time. You are teaching little human beings, who have not had any need to control their bodily functions, to *hold* their urges until they get to the potty. This does not happen overnight, but it can happen within three to four days, so stay committed. You may not have any sign that they are getting it today, but you will soon. Continue to cheer them on, staying positive and excited when they finish on the potty. Treats are a perfect addition to training when a peepee or poop actually lands in the potty.

Day Three: Don't Put the White Flag Up: the Breakthrough Begins!

Okay, you are almost there! Are you still smiling? Wake up and get dressed and ready for your day prior to the babies waking up, if possible. Today you will follow the exact same procedure as for day two. During the day today, you should see more recognition by your children of the relationship of their elimination and the potty. Stay on top of them, watch them carefully, and get them to the potty as soon as they start peeing or pooping. Cheer, sing, dance, and continue to be happy and supportive. This should be a day filled with new activities and new treats. Draw, read new books, play hide-and-seek and other games. Remember to have your children mutually support each other by cheering and clapping with you when their sibling uses the potty. By the end of today, at least one of your babies will be telling you he needs to potty at the time he is starting or before. It will all come together for both of them by tomorrow, if it hasn't yet. My experience has shown that if this program is followed diligently and carefully, your babies will be going to the potty on their own by day four. Of course, every situation presents its own challenges that might get in the way. Be creative. Stay positive. Look for solutions.

Today is a good day to start a little game called the "Listening Game." When you put them on their potty, tilt your head, put your finger to your ear, and say, "Let's listen." Then quietly wait for a tinkle or a plop, and say, "Did you hear that? You just went peepee. Yeah!" And when you get a plop, say "Plop! Did you hear that? You pooped!" This will help you get them to concentrate on what they were doing instead of doodling around, looking at stickers, pulling the toilet paper off the roll, talking to their sibling, etc. I still used this technique six months later when we were out in public places to get them to focus on the task at hand. (The less time spent in a public restroom, the better.) It makes children laugh, and it makes them very proud of themselves when they can hear a tinkle or a plop.

Please don't compare your babies. Unless they are identical, they are completely different individuals. One may get it faster than the other. If that happens, it may become frustrating for you when the other one continues to have accidents. *Don't let it get to you.* Keep the same patience and support that you started with, and know that the other one will start to get it soon. Today is the day when they should both start to catch on. Keep the faith.

In review, stay on the same schedule as you have for day one and day two. Continue with plenty of healthy snacks and liquids, and use treats when your babies accomplish their business on the potty. Stay focused, positive, and supportive, constantly communicating how proud you are of your babies.

Day Four: Success: The Battle Is Won!

By today, both of your babies should be grasping the concept of using the potty, and you should be proud of yourself and your twins. Start today just like the last three days: same program, but it should be getting easier. Don't get too relaxed, though. It is very important for you to keep the same focus today as you have maintained the last three days. I know, you really want to get out of the house, but don't do it, except for maybe a walk around the block after your twins have successfully used the potty. This is the day it should all fall into place if it has not already. Continue the process by asking if they need to use the potty on a regular basis, placing them on the potty before and after meals and bedtime, and praising them for every little accomplishment. Although there have been many accidents over the last three day, and you are probably totally exhausted, you should be seeing the beginning of a "diaper-free" world.

By the end of today, your twins should be consistently telling you when they need to potty or taking themselves to the potty. By tomorrow you will be able to venture out of the house with your little ones.

Day Five: Graduation Day: Get Out and Celebrate!

Congratulations, today is graduation day! You have successfully completed *Potty Training Boot Camp for Twins*. Get out and celebrate with ice cream or cupcakes, and revel in the fact that your twins are potty trained at such an early age.

Continue to consistently use the tools and processes you have used over the last four days and *make sure* to implement "Part III: After Boot Camp" to stay on track with your new routine. Now you can confidently share with your friends and family what you and your babies have accomplished, and they will be amazed!

Part III:
After Boot Camp

Staying on Track for the Next Few Weeks

Keep at least one potty close at hand in your home for the first few weeks after Boot Camp, and slowly move it into the bathroom. If it is in view, it will serve as a reminder for your busy twins. Always say, "It's potty time!" and lead your children to the potty before and after meals and bedtime and when you arrive or depart anywhere. Do not ask, "Do you need to go potty?" at these specific times. These times aren't up for discussion. These are habits that need to be formed. I will tell you that a busy toddler will not answer "yes" to this question very often. This is when the bribery starts. Yes, I know, none of us wants to do it, but it will be necessary at this time of your life. The need for the bribery goes away after a couple of months, but for now, find a little treat that your children like and give it to them when you need them to try to use the potty. I carried all-natural gummy bears that you can get at health food stores, and the babies got one when they used the potty at these times. It is totally worth giving your children a gummy bear to pee before a trip in the car so that they are dry when you pick them up out of the car seat. Don't feel guilty. Just know that the need will fade over time, and habits will become established without any bribery needed. A few gummy bears never hurt anyone. (They make sugar-free ones, if that is a concern.)

Try to always plan on being someplace fifteen minutes early. That way, if there is an accident, you are not completely stressed due to a time frame. This policy will give you time to calmly address the situation, clean your toddler up, change her clothes, and still get to your destination on time. Put your children in clothing that is potty training friendly. No one-pieces, overalls, etc. Keep them in two-piece clothing or a dress. I kept my daughter in shorts and pants for the first couple of months, as it seemed a lot easier to change one piece of clothing than a whole outfit if we did have an accident.

Nap and Night Training

If your children have not been waking up from their naps dry, keep them in the training undies for a little while longer. Try to limit their liquid intake forty-five minutes to one hour before their nap. This should help with the process. When they consistently start waking up dry, it is time to let the training undies go. Have a conversation with them, and ask them if they can stay dry during their nap. Get very excited when they wake up dry. My children just told me one day that they wanted to wear their undies at nap time, and that was that.

I recommend Pull-Ups (remember to call them "nighttime undies," *not* "diapers") at night after day training, until they are consistently waking up dry. My children were trained during the night by two and a half years. We live in a dry climate, and I had a hard time telling them they could not have water at night before bed, so we made adjustments. We would put them to bed at eight o'clock and right before we went to bed at ten, we would quietly get them out of bed and put them on the potty. They would use it and wake up dry the next morning. Our children were still in cribs, so we would carry them to the potty and carry them back to bed. They would go right back down. You can let your children know at night that you will wake them up before you go to bed so that they can go potty and stay dry. If your children are consistently dry during their nap, but wet in the mornings, try this schedule, as it should make a difference. We followed this program until they were about three years old. Create a system that works for you and your twins.

Accidents Will Happen

Always carry extra wipes, undies, pants, and socks (yes, they get wet too) just in case. I can't stress this enough. There is nothing worse than getting somewhere, you can't get your daughter to pee on the potty, and five minutes later she has peed in her pants and you have nothing to change her into. Also, keep a supply on hand of the little diaper bags you carry for poopy diapers for accidents to put the wet/dirty undies into. Some children may have an accident a week; some may have a couple a day for a while. You will see this taper off, but they are just learning the control and the habit of heading to the potty when they feel the urge. One of my most memorable accidents was when the kids and I went to the bookstore to purchase some Christmas gifts. They had been trained for about a month. I didn't take them to the potty when we arrived, and about fifteen minutes later, my daughter was standing in the middle of the children's reading area with pee streaming down her legs and a puddle under her shoes . . . on the carpet! I was so embarrassed. I promptly picked up both my children and walked out of the store *without* telling a soul! How wrong is that? I just couldn't bear the thought of someone looking at me and my child in complete disgust, so I just snuck out. (Of course, that industrial-strength carpet is made for wear and tear and spills. I am sure it cleaned up just fine!)

Stay excited about their progress. Continue to praise them for the next several months for using the potty and for waking up dry every time. My children had been in undies for almost a year, and I still clapped and cheered and told them how proud I was that they used the potty. A few accidents can deliver a major blow to a toddler's self-esteem. Make a conscious effort to recognize the achievement when they do reach the potty in time. Increase your children's self-confidence by letting them know how proud you are of their other achievements: getting their clothes on themselves, the pictures they painted, washing their hands before dinner, etc. The better they feel about themselves, the better their chances of making it to the potty next time.

When You Are Out and About

When you are out running errands, know where the nearest potty is; you may have to get there quickly. I highly recommend having your portable potty with you on outings. If you have been out for a while, make sure you stop at the restroom when you arrive somewhere. Keep in mind when your children are eating and drinking and when they will probably need to use the potty. I find that a lot of accidents can be avoided if you stay active in keeping on top of how long it has been since your children used the bathroom. When you are at someone's home, make sure you know where the guest bath is, and make sure your children know where the potty is. The first thing I did when I went to someone's home was to take my children to the bathroom. If your host has small children, there will probably be a little potty there. If not, I used to take our potty seat with us. When we traveled to visit friends and family, I always took the potty seat and a stool in my suitcase. I also always carried some gummy bears with me to entice them to use the potty. After your children have been trained for a few months, it usually becomes unnecessary to bribe them, but it's always nice to be prepared, because sometimes they are stubborn!

Resisting the Urge to Tidy Up

Relinquish your power. Let your toddlers do their potty deeds themselves if that is what they want. If they want help, help them, but if your little girl says, "Kayla do it!" let her do it. You can send a negative message by letting your children know, through actions, that the things they are doing are not done quite right. Your child might be slow at getting her pants down, and you jump in and help. Your son might hit the seat or the floor because he looks away, and you reach over and adjust his stance. You might tend to push them to hurry up if you are trying to get out the door or are in a public restroom. When they pull their pants up, they might be crooked, and you reach over and fix them. They may pull too much toilet paper and not wipe the right way.

All of this "helping" might seem innocent on the surface, but by doing this you are sending your children the message that they are not doing things quite right. Just let them do the best they can; that is what it is all about. Tell your son to try to keep it in the potty, and praise him when he does. Pee wipes up with a little vinegar water and paper towels, so don't sweat it when it happens. He will learn to hit the target. If your daughter insists on wiping herself, work on the proper technique of front-to-back wipes when she poops. Praise her and tell her what a great job she did wiping, and then say, "Mommy is just going to do a final booty wipe. You did great, and you are such a big girl." Be aware of how your actions can affect your children's confidence.

Getting Rid of the Baby Potty

I recommend keeping the training potties available until your children no longer have the desire to use them. They are typically bonded to their potties for a while, so don't take them away too soon. You also need to feel comfortable with your children stepping on a stool and then placing themselves on the adult toilet without falling off. Sometimes my children preferred the little potty, and sometimes they liked to sit on the Elmo or Dora potty seats. If your toddlers always want to go on the adult toilet, you can probably say bye-bye to the little potty. We had a training potty in our guest bath and the babies' bathroom until they were about three and a half, with potty top seats and stools in each of the additional baths. My precious little daughter thought it was really funny to pretend that she was falling in the potty if she didn't have a potty seat on top and dunk her bottom in the toilet water (yuck!), so I kept those around for a while. Do whatever feels right for you and your children, but I think it is nice to have both options in the bathrooms that they use most often, as they both sit on the potty at the same time before you leave the house, when you return, and before and after naps and bedtime.

Dealing with Parents in Separate Homes

Divorce is a tough enough experience in and of itself without bringing potty training into the equation. Your ex needs to be on board for this to work. Discuss this with him before starting the process. Share this book with him. Get the same potty chairs, potty tops, and stools for both homes. You can be in charge of the boot camp, but he needs to follow the process and commit to no more diapers and the accidents that often come with it. If he thinks "diapers are easier," then you will just be shooting yourself in the foot by starting this process. You need to agree to work on this together. Communicate with your children and tell them, "When you are at Daddy's house, won't it be fun to show him how big you are and how you can use the potty now?"

Please note the following instructions when dealing with potty training with your ex:

- Never shift blame if your child has an accident. Assume, if he tells you so, that your ex is sticking with the plan.
- Stay cool. Discuss the progress and any issues.
- Resolve problems. If you both stick with it and stay consistent, there won't be accidents for long.
- Say "thanks" for working on this together.

Dealing with Day Care

First and foremost, make sure your daycare provider is on board before you start the training. If the day care you use is not accepting of this program, you will need to find one that is. Most good providers are happy to keep your child on track, as long as you explain to them exactly what they need to do. Telling your caregiver your expectations at the beginning is much better than backtracking.

On your first day back to day care after training, arrive early and express to them, "My children are now potty trained, and we are so excited! I need your support to ensure that they continue to do well. Please, while I am at work, follow this schedule for my children. Here is what I need you to do . . ." Make sure they understand your expectations up front. Show them the "potty" sign, and make sure they understand how to use it and what it looks like when your children use it. Give them a schedule of when to check on your children to see if they will use the potty. For example, thirty minutes after they drink any liquid, right after they eat their snack or lunch, before and after they nap, etc. Type it up and hang it on the wall with your children's names on it. Don't assume they will remember. Make sure they understand to use a lot of praise and to never get upset with them if they have an accident. My little boy had no problem telling people when he needed to go, but my little girl would get busy and forget. Always send their special "potty treats" and a change of clothes with extra undies and socks to day care, just in case.

An example of a schedule for your daycare provider would be:

1. Take her to the potty after meals and snacks and thirty minutes after any liquids. Bribe her with a "potty treat." If she refuses, don't push it. Give her praise for doing a good job trying, and try again in twenty minutes.
2. Ask her several times throughout the day to tell you when she needs to go, and use the potty sign. "Can you tell me when you need to go to the potty?"
3. Let her pull up her own pants, and don't fix them for her.
4. Tell her what a great job she did and what a big girl she is when she uses the potty.
5. Don't make her feel guilty if she has an accident. Clean her up, put new clothes on her, and say, "I know you will use the potty next time, because you are such a big girl!"
6. Remember to use the potty sign, and make sure you are watching for her signing it to you.

This type of information is imperative, as everyone has their own thoughts on potty training, and you want your children's training to stay consistent.

A daycare program may have ten to twenty children in a classroom, so they will definitely need something on the wall to remind them to focus on your children for the first few weeks after training. If your daycare provider is an individual, have her read over the directions and make sure she can repeat back to you what she is going to be responsible for. If your daycare provider is a preschool, inform the director of your expectations. Talk to the teachers in the classroom, and make sure each of them understands their responsibilities to keep your children on track. In either environment, spend some time over the first couple of days your child is back, and watch to make sure the provider gets it and can successfully carry through the training.

Toilet Training Setbacks

Sometimes a toddler who has been using the potty for weeks or months has a setback. Accidents will happen, but if it becomes a regular occurrence, there is usually a reason.

A new routine: If a daycare situation has changed, preschool has started, or your children's typical routine has changed, your children may have trouble adapting or feel uncomfortable about using a different toilet. To be proactive regarding this type of setback, take your children to the new school or day care a couple of times before you leave them for their first day. Make sure they know where the potty is and that it is okay to tell their teacher or childcare provider when they need to use it. Speak to your childcare provider or preschool teacher to make sure they understand your children's potty routine and remind your children to use the potty. Ask them to give some extra attention to your little ones for a couple of weeks until they become comfortable with their new situation. If you have been rushing out the door in the morning to get them to their new day care/school, get up earlier and give your children more time to use the potty after breakfast and again when you get to their destination. Sometimes a little walk after breakfast can guarantee potty success before you leave the house.

Stress: A new sibling, a new teacher, a new babysitter, or travel can emotionally upset a child. Changes in those around them can cause confusion and emotional discomfort. Reduce the stress as much as possible. Make sure the new teacher or babysitter is the right fit for your children, understands your children's routine, and will remind them to use the potty. Make sure your children are getting enough affection and attention now that a new baby is in the house. Ensure some one-on-one time with your toddlers on a regular basis so that they know you love spending time with them alone, as well as with the whole family. When traveling, try to keep their daily schedule — as far as naps and meals are concerned — as routine as possible. Take your portable potty with you so that they have their own little potty to use in the airport, airplane, etc. The auto-flush toilets and airplane toilets can terrify a small child. When staying in a new place, make sure your toddlers know where the bathroom is, and have their potty seat and stool in place when they want to use the toilet. Potty seats and stools pack easily in a suitcase and are worth taking with you. I took mine every time we traveled.

Anger: A child that is angry with his parents may decide to strike back by using his undies, because he knows it upsets them. Don't blink an eye, and don't do any name calling! Reacting to the accident is exactly what your child is looking for. Respond casually and supportively: "Oops, you had an accident. That's okay, we all have accidents. Next time I know you will make it to the potty, because you are such a big girl! Let's get you cleaned up." And clean her up and give her a big hug. If she is willing (but do not force her), foster grown-up feelings by getting her to help you clean up the mess and change her clothes. Never respond to any accidents by saying things like "I thought you were a big girl," or "Do I need to put you back in diapers?" This will *not* encourage grown-up behavior or have a positive impact on your child.

Constipation: If a child is constipated, bowel movements may be painful, and she may develop a fear of going to the potty. She may hold her bowel movement for as long as she can, until it can wait no more, and then have an accident. Make sure that your children are getting enough fiber with fruits, vegetables, and grains, and plenty of fluids, especially water, and exercise. Fresh fruit (especially pears and apples), dried fruit, fresh and steamed vegetables, beans, peas, wild rice, rolled oats, and bran flakes are easy and necessary parts of a healthy fiber-filled diet. Toddlers should be getting at least a quart to a quart and a half of fluids a day. Make sure your children are drinking plenty of water throughout the day, with milk and juice at meals or snack time. Limit cow's milk to three cups a day, as the calcium salts can harden stools. One hundred percent unfiltered apple juice (available at health food stores) is very helpful at battling constipation. Make sure your children are getting plenty of activity every day and not spending extensive amounts of time in the car or stroller. If you are on a road trip by car, make sure breaks include some outdoor play in the countryside, or an indoor play area or pool.

Loose stools: Softer bowel movements come out quicker and with less ability to control. Diarrhea can be caused by a variety of things, including a virus, bacteria, an allergy, an infection, a change in diet, or too much fruit juice. If you suspect an illness or allergy, visit your doctor. If you suspect diet, offer your child plenty of water, but limit fruit juices to once a day, and try to get them back on their regular diet. Do not give your child soda or athletic drinks.

Urinary tract infections: These are more common in girls and can be caused by bubble baths, bath oils, and harsh bath soaps and detergents. Urinating may hurt, only come out a little bit at a time, and be hard to control. If your child's urine is cloudy, pink, or blood-tinged, get her to the doctor.

No apparent explanation: Sometimes children just have a setback. Maybe they just decide it is more convenient every once in a while to use their undies than go to the potty. You may have very busy children, like my daughter who sometimes just couldn't be bothered to run to the potty in a timely manner. This issue takes some creative thinking on your part. Accidents may be happening on a daily basis or once a week. You don't know why, and your children have no explanation. My daughter went through a phase at about thirty-one months of age. She had been totally accident-free for a couple of months, and all of a sudden she just decided she was too busy to go to the potty to poop on a regular basis. A couple of times a week, she would just use her undies—no big deal in her eyes, as her mommy would help clean her up. Then, the first day of the swim season arrived. I put swim Pull-Ups on her, and after her swim she decided to poop in them! Unbelievable, but I decided this was an opportune moment in time. I knew she loved the water. I promptly cleaned her up, dressed her, and told her we were going home. "Only big girls who go in the potty *all* the time get to go swimming. Girls who poopoo in their undies are not allowed in the swimming pool." I wasn't mean or condescending, just matter-of-fact. We left the pool, and she was not happy. (And, yes, her brother came with us.) The next day, I asked her if she wanted to go swimming. She said "yes." I said, "Only big girls who poopoo in the potty *all* the time get to go swimming. Can you poopoo in the potty today?" "Yes, Mommy." "Okay, then we will go swimming!" And then I would remind her at the pool, and every day thereafter for about two weeks. There was not another day that arrived that she pooped in her undies. So, for you, figure out something that is very important to them, and explain that big boys and girls get to do that and that big boys and girls *always* use the potty. Stand strong on restricting this activity/privilege/game if they do not respond. Be matter-of-fact, don't make them feel bad, and just give them the choice.

In Conclusion

You should be proud of your accomplishment, and I hope you feel the result has been worth it. One of my favorite comments from others that I experienced while walking the kids to the potty during their second year was: "Oh, are you starting potty training?" And I would proudly announce, "Oh no, they have been potty trained since before they were two!" And the looks of disbelief were so much fun. It made every little accident worth it. Maybe it's just in my world, but having twins who were potty trained before two was pretty amazing to most people. My husband thanked me again right before the kids' third birthday. He had been in their preschool and was amazed at all the three-year-olds still in diapers. How quickly we forget the dirty diapers. I had to change the diaper of an almost-three-year-old friend, and that poop was all over the place. It was times like those that made me so thankful to have my kiddos in undies!

Congratulations on your success and the success of your babies! You should be extremely proud of yourself and your children.

Potty Training Boot Camp Cheat Sheet

One Month Before Training

- Begin teaching your child the American Sign Language sign for "potty." Use this every day and every time you have a chance. Your children *must* be proficient in the use of this sign before starting training. *This program will not work unless you and your children are proficient and comfortable with consistently using the "potty" sign.*
- Schedule your time off from work.

Two Weeks Before Training

- Stop all potty training techniques that you have been using. Let them use the potty if they choose to, but do not do any type of training.
- Purchase all of the supplies you will need.
- Understand their pooping schedule.

Two Days Before Training

- Take your toddlers to pick out their big-kid undies.
- Make sure you have everything you need for the program.
- Make sure all meals have been made for the four-day program, or have plans ready for delivery.

- Wrap up your workload.
- Get your training area in your home ready to go. Move out any valuable rugs or furniture your children may sit on.

Day One of Training

- Throw away all diapers for your little ones.
- You will be running your children to the potty all day with a lot of accidents. Keep up the signing of "potty" and all of the excitement.
- Begin the schedule of putting them on the potty before and after nap and bedtime and before and after meals.
- No treats on this day.

Day Two of Training:

- Same as day one, but you can start using some treats if they finish a peepee or poopoo on the potty.
- You will probably feel no sense of accomplishment by the end of today, but keep up the spirit and stay strong.

Day Three of Training

- Same as days one and two, but by the end of this day you should start seeing some signing of "potty" from at least one of your children when they are starting to go or are about to go.
- This day should have all new toys and games.
- If you see the sign or hear the word "potty" when your child starts to pee or poop, your child is starting

to associate the feeling of peeing or pooping with the word/sign "potty" and trips to the potty, and this is a huge accomplishment.

- Start playing the "Listening Game."
- Keep up the excitement and the treats for accomplishments.
- Don't give up; this is the hardest day of all.

Day Four of Training

- This is the day it all comes together, so stay strong, excited, and positive!
- Your toddlers will be signing on a regular basis before they need to go to the potty and heading to the potty on their own by the end of the day.
- Stay excited, positive, and full of energy and praise for your babies.

Day Five of Training

- This is graduation day! Both of your children should be signing when they need to go to the potty.
- Maintain the schedule of putting them on the potty before and after nap and bedtime, and before and a Get your training fter meals.
- Get out of the house for a little while to celebrate!
- Remember to put them on the potty before and after you take a car ride or leave the house.

Staying on Track

- Put together a schedule for your daycare provider.

- Take your portable potty seat wherever you go. Have it ready for your babies when they need it.
- Always take a change of clothes, including socks.
- Always take "potty treats" with you.
- Give yourself an extra fifteen minutes to get anywhere.
- Stay consistent, calm, and positive.
- Always take your child to the bathroom as soon as you arrive anywhere and before you leave.
- Know where the nearest bathroom is when you are out and about.
- Remember to praise all of their accomplishments, and resist the urge to tidy up.

Encouraging Phrases for Training

Before Training Starts

"We are going to start wearing big-kid undies soon. Won't that be fun? We aren't going to wear baby diapers anymore, because we are going to learn to peepee and poopoo on the potty like Mommy and Daddy. See your potties? Won't they be fun to use?"

"See our new big-kid undies and our potties. How cool are those, Daddy?"

"We are going to say bye-bye to our diapers, and we are going to start wearing our big-kid undies! You two are so big!"

"Bye-bye, diapers. Let's put our big-kid undies on! Won't that be fun?"

During Training

"Let's go to the potty! Yeah! You went peepee on the potty. You are so big!"

"Yeah, sweetie, you just pooped in the potty. You are so big! Oh my goodness, look at that poop! Do you see it? Wow! Do you want to flush it down? Bye-bye, poopoo!"

"What a great try!"

"Okay, let's finish on the potty! I bet next time you will make it to the potty in time because you are such a big boy!"

"You almost did it. You are so big! Mommy is so proud of you! Let's finish on the potty. What a big girl!"

"Let's go potty!"

Throughout Training and for Several Months After

"You peeped on the potty. You are so big! I am so proud of you!"

"I hear that! Did you just poop on the potty? You are so big!"

"Let's take our nighttime undies off and go peepee in the potty!"

"It's time for our nap. Let's sit on the potty and go peepee so we will be dry when we wake up."

Play the Listening Game. When you put them on their potty, tilt your head, put your finger to your ear, and say, "Let's listen . . ." And quietly wait for a tinkle or a plop and say, "Did you hear that? You just went peepee. Yeah!" And when you get a plop, say, "Plop! Did you hear that? You pooped!"

Always say, "It's potty time!" and lead them to the potty before and after meals and bedtime and when you arrive or depart anywhere.

When Accidents Occur

Never make your child feel guilty: "Okay, let's finish on the potty! I bet next time you will make it to the potty in time because you are such a big boy!"

The most important thing is to always stay positive, always praise, and *never* reprimand your children for having an accident. They have only just started to learn their responsibilities in this crazy world we live in. Think about it. They have been on this earth for less than two years. Give them as much love, support, patience, and praise as you can give, and you will have two beautifully potty trained toddlers before the age of two.

References

Bakker, Wilhelmina. *Research into the Influence of Potty Training on Lower Urinary Tract Dysfunction.* Antwerp, Belgium: University of Antwerp, 2002.

Brazelton, T. Berry. "A Child-Oriented Approach to Toilet Training." *Pediatrics* 29 (1962): 121-28.

Maizels, Max, Kevin Gandhy, Barbara Keating, and Diane Rosenbaum. "Diagnosis and Treatment for Children Who Cannot Control Urination." *Current Problems in Pediatrics* 10 (1993): 402-50.

Partsch, C. J., M. Aukamp, and W. G. Sippell. "Scrotal Temperature Is Increased in Disposable Plastic Lined Nappies." *Archives of Disease in Childhood* 83 (2000): 364-68.

Schmitt, Barton D. "Toilet Training Problems: Underachievers, Refusers, and Stool Holders." *Contemporary Pediatrics* 21, no. 4 (April 2004): 71-82.

Schonwald, Alison, Lon Sherrit, Ann Stadtler, and Carolyn Bridgemohan. "Factors Associated with Difficult Toilet Training." *Pediatrics* 113 (2004): 1753-57.

Schum, Timothy R., T. L. McAuliffe, M. D. Simms, J. A. Walter, M. Lewis, and R. Rupp. "Factors Associated with Toilet Training in the 1990s." *Ambulatory Pediatrics* 1 (2001): 79-86.